Why do elephants trumpet?

camilla de la Bedoyere

Miles
Kelly

First published in 2011 by Miles Kelly Publishing Ltd
Harding's Barn, Bardfield End Green, Thaxted,
Essex, CM6 3PX, UK

2 4 6 8 10 9 7 5 3 1

Publishing Director Belinda Gallagher
Creative Director Jo Cowan
Editorial Director Rosie McGuire
Editor Carly Blake
Volume Designer Greg Best
Cover Designer Kayleigh Allen
Image Manager Liberty Newton
Indexer Gill Lee
Production Manager Elizabeth Collins
Reprographics Antony Cambray, Stephan Davis

ISBN 978-1-84810-456-3

Printed in China

British Library Cataloguing-in-Publication Data

A catalogue record for this book is
available from the British Library

ACKNOWLEDGEMENTS
The publishers would like to thank the following
artists who have contributed to this book:

Ian Jackson (cover), Mike Foster (character cartoons)

All other artwork from the Miles Kelly Artwork Bank

The publishers would like to thank the following
sources for the use of their photographs:

Fotolia.com 20 TMAX; 23 Bhupi; 29 granitepeaker
Getty 24 Barcroft Media via Getty Images
Moviestore Collection 17 © Walt Disney Productions
Shutterstock.com 6 Josep Pena Llorens; 9 Four Oaks;
16 Igor Janicek; 17 Johan Swanepoel; 19 Carole Castelli;
25 Igor Zakowski
Topfoto 26 The Granger Collection

All other photographs are from:
Corel, digitalSTOCK, digitalvision, John Foxx, PhotoAlto,
PhotoDisc, PhotoEssentials, PhotoPro, Stockbyte

Every effort has been made to acknowledge the
source and copyright holder of each picture.
Miles Kelly Publishing apologises for any unintentional
errors or omissions.

Made with paper from a sustainable forest

www.mileskelly.net
info@mileskelly.net

www.factsforprojects.com

Self-publish your
children's book

buddingpress.co.uk

contents

were mammoths woolly?

Woolly mammoth →

Yes, they had long, woolly fur to keep them warm in freezing weather. Mammoths were relatives of modern elephants and they lived thousands of years ago, when the world was much colder. Early people hunted mammoths for food, and for their thick fur.

How do we know about mammoths?

Because we have found their bodies frozen in ice. The freezing temperatures allowed the bones, hair and skin of some mammoths to remain almost the same for thousands of years.

Ancient art!

Long ago, people lived in caves. They painted animals, including mammoths, on the stone walls of their caves.

Paint

Make your own cave art. Paint mammoths, bears and wolves onto a big piece of strong paper or card.

Did elephants live with dinosaurs?

No, elephants came along millions of years after dinosaurs. The earliest elephants were a family of animals that looked like big pigs with long noses. Over time these animals changed and became the elephants we know today.

Early elephants

why are elephants so big?

Being big helps elephants to reach lots of tasty leaves in the trees. It also keeps them safe – not many animals would dare to attack such a huge beast! Elephants are the biggest animals that live on land, but their closest relatives are animals no bigger than rabbits.

Safari jeep

Wild African elephant

Do elephants have families?

Yes, and their family groups are called herds. A herd is made up of baby elephants and their mothers, aunts and grandmothers. The oldest female elephant is in charge of the herd. Adult male elephants live alone.

Herd of elephants

Greedy guts!
Elephants have to spend most of the day eating. They munch up to 200 kilograms of grass, leaves, flowers and fruits every day.

what is a baby elephant called?

A baby elephants is called a calf. Elephant calves are playful and they have lots of things to learn, such as how to use their trunks. They stay close to their mothers until they are around four years old.

Find out
What animals will these babies grow up to be?
Kitten Puppy
Lamb Gosling

7

Are all elephants the same?

No, there are three different types. Two live in Africa and one lives in Asia. African bush elephants live in grasslands. African forest elephants have hairy trunks and dark skin, and live in forests. Asian elephants are smaller than their African relatives and have smaller ears.

Asian elephants are 2 to 3.5 metres tall

African elephants can be 4 metres tall

Compare

Use a measuring tape to see how tall African and Asian elephants are. How tall are you?

How do baby elephants grow so strong?

They drink their mothers' milk – the perfect food for growing babies. A calf puts on up to 5 kilograms in weight every day. That is the same as five bags of sugar!

Calf drinking its mother's milk

Why do elephants pick up sticks?

Elephants pick up sticks with their trunks and use them to flick flies away, in the same way that humans use fly swats. Some elephants also use sticks to play with, scratch their backs or to doodle in the sand!

Underwater!

Baby elephants can swim almost as soon as they can walk. They can even suckle (drink their mother's milk) while underwater.

Why do elephants trumpet?

To talk to each other. An elephant makes a loud trumpeting sound by blasting air through its trunk. This tells other elephants that it is angry, scared or excited. Elephants also use rumbles, snorts and groans to 'talk' to each other.

Trunk

Do elephants get itchy?

Yes, especially if they have ticks. These little bugs suck their blood, making their skin sore. Elephants rub against trees until the ticks fall off. They also use their trunks to blow dust over their skin to stop the ticks biting.

scratch

Try scratching like an elephant. Rub your back against the edge of a door. Did it work?

Elephant rubbing on a tree

How do elephants help vets?

Elephants can help vets (animal doctors) get close to dangerous wild animals. When a rhino is ill, it is more likely to attack. By sitting on an elephant's back, a vet can get close enough to give it medical care.

Trumpet!

An elephant can trumpet so loudly that its call can be heard up to 10 kilometres away.

Do angry elephants flap their ears?

Yes, this is one way elephants show each other that they are not happy. Angry elephants also stamp the ground and shake their heads. This warns other animals – and people – to go away, or face big trouble!

Two elephants fighting

Try

Look in the mirror and see if you can move your ears without touching them. It might take practise!

Why are tusks like weapons?

Male elephants use their tusks like weapons to fight each other. Tusks are just overgrown teeth, but a stab from one can be deadly. The elephant with the biggest tusks usually wins the battle.

Get out of the way!

When a group of elephants run, it is called a stampede. A herd of stampeding elephants tramples anything in its path.

When do calves start to walk?

Elephant calves can walk when they are just 30 minutes old. The baby grows inside its mother for nearly two years. At birth, a calf is one metre tall and weighs the same as a man!

can people ride on elephants?

Yes, they can. Asian elephants can learn to follow commands to work with people and carry tourists through the jungle. This gives local people jobs and teaches them to care about elephants. In the future, it is hoped that all elephants can be returned to the wild.

Tourists riding on elephants

why do people paint elephants?

In Asia, elephants are considered very important, so people decorate them for festivals and celebrations. They are painted in bright colours, or dressed with beautiful fabrics and jewels.

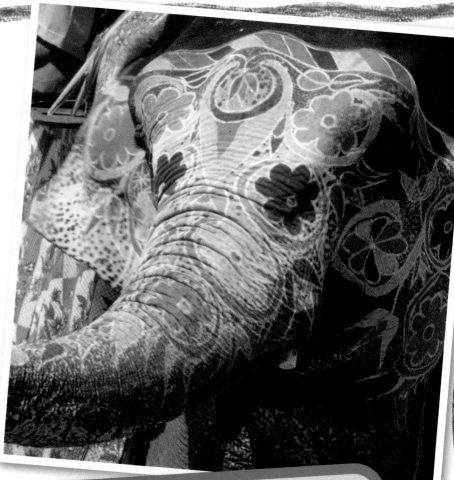

Elephant decorated with paint

Timber!

In some places, elephants are losing their forest homes. Many trees are cut down so that farmers can use the land to grow more crops.

How much do elephants weigh?

A lot! Male African elephants can weigh up to 6 tonnes. That is the same as about 80 people! A male weighs the same as two females. Asian elephants weigh less than African elephants.

work out

If a male African elephant weighs 6 tonnes, how much does a female weigh?

where do elephants go to drink?

Elephants walk a long way to find places to drink called waterholes. These are dips in the ground where water collects. Elephants drink what they need, and splash around to stay cool. Like other animal visitors to the waterhole, elephants graze on plants that grow nearby.

Giraffe

Elephant

Zebras

Waterhole

Dung balls!

Elephants make about 20 kilograms of dung (poo) a day. Dung beetles roll the dung into balls, and lay their eggs in them.

Mould

Use plasticine to mould an elephant. Stand it on some foil for water – like it's at a waterhole.

which elephant can fly?

Dumbo can! He is a young elephant in the Disney movie. As a baby, Dumbo gets teased by the other elephants in the circus because he has huge ears. In the end, Dumbo realizes he can fly using his ears as wings.

why do elephants roll in mud?

Elephants like to get covered in mud because it protects their skin from the Sun. It also stops insects from biting. Once elephants have cooled off in the waterhole, they often roll in mud at the edge and get dirty again!

Elephant splashing in the *mud*

17

Are trunks sensitive?

Yes – they are super-sized noses that can pick objects up. Elephants also use their trunks to communicate. They put their trunks in each other's mouths to say 'hello'. Mothers gently stroke their calves with their trunks to reassure them and to bond with them.

Mother and calf touching trunks

Do elephants have teeth?

Yes, they do. An elephant's teeth are big and strong – one tooth can be bigger than a man's shoe! An elephant has six sets of teeth during its life – a human only has two.

count

How many teeth do you have? Find out how many teeth grown-ups have too. Who has more?

An elephant's back teeth →

can elephants hear with their feet?

Yes they can. Elephants make deep rumbling sounds, which travel through the ground. Other elephants feel the sounds with their feet. The sounds travel through the elephants' bones to its ears, so they can hear the noise.

Toothless!

Older elephants may die when their last set of teeth wears out because they can no longer eat.

Are elephants smart?

Elephants are very smart, and they can learn new skills. Some Asian elephants have learnt how to hold paintbrushes in their trunks and paint pictures! Others have worked out how to turn on taps, open gates and whistle.

Learn

Can you learn a new skill? Try painting a picture – but holding the brush in your mouth!

Asian elephant painting →

African
elephant's
trunk

HOW long is an elephant's trunk?

Male African elephants have the longest trunks, growing to 2 metres in length. That's about the same as a man's height! African elephants have two tips on the end of their trunk, but Asian elephants only have one tip.

Ta-da!

In the past, elephants were trained to perform tricks in circuses. They have also been used to carry heavy loads into war.

Skunk

Do elephants smell well?

Yes! An elephant's trunk can smell other animals from far away. They hold their trunks up high to sniff the air. Male elephants also use their sense of smell to find females at mating time.

Why do elephants chew bark?

Chewing bark takes hours, but it is full of goodness. Grass tastes better, but when there is not much around, elephants eat bark, branches and even roots. Some trees are poisonous and calves learn not to eat them by copying their mothers and aunts.

Elephant chewing bark

Think
Vegetables are foods that are full of goodness. How many different types can you think of?

which birds stand on elephants?

Birds called egrets stand on elephants' heads to enjoy some tasty snacks! Egrets feast on the flies and other bugs that buzz around elephants. The elephants don't mind the birds because they get rid of their annoying pests!

Egret

Don't make me mad!

An angry elephant uses its tusks to attack and stab. A single elephant is so strong that it could flip a car over with its tusks!

Do elephants chase animals?

Sometimes an elephant will chase an animal away if it feels scared by it. A mother elephant may charge if she thinks her calf is in danger. Angry adult elephants have been know to kill baboons, lions and even people.

Charging elephant

Baboon

Do elephants go swimming?

Even though they are huge, elephants are good swimmers. They use their trunks like snorkels, so they can breathe air even when their heads are underwater. Some elephants roll right over so only their feet poke out of the water.

Elephant swimming

Find out

The biggest animal in the world is an excellent swimmer. Can you find out what it is?

Why do elephants have big ears?

Elephants live in hot countries and big ears help them to cool down. As they gently flap their ears, the moving air cools the blood inside. The cooled blood then moves around the rest of the elephant's body.

Do elephants remember?

They seem to. When elephants pass the bones of one of their herd, they stop and touch them with their trunks. They seem to be remembering their relative. Elephants can also remember where waterholes are and where to find good food.

Hello baby!

Newborn calves are welcomed into their family. All members come close and touch the baby gently, so it can get to know them all.

Elephants touching bones

Which huge elephant was famous?

Jumbo was the most famous elephant ever, and one of the largest. He was captured in 1861 and kept in zoos and a circus. Jumbo reached 4 metres in height! This is why people use the word 'jumbo' to mean big.

Jumbo the elephant

why do elephants march?

Elephants go on long walks, or marches, to look for food and water. After a rainy season, herds march to places where they know the plants they eat will be growing. Walking in a big group also helps to keep the herd safe from predators.

Mmm...salty!

Some elephants walk into caves searching for salt, which they lick off the cave walls! Salt is a mineral that elephants need to keep healthy.

Make

Ask an adult to help you cut an elephant shape out of card with four holes where its legs are. Put your fingers through the holes to make it march!

Is elephant dung tasty?

To some animals it is! Elephant dung is full of plants that haven't been digested (broken down). Animals such as baboons, warthogs and birds sort through the dung to find seeds, grass and pieces of fruit to eat.

Baboon eating elephant dung →

Do mothers protect their babies?

Yes, mother elephants guard their calves. Sometimes calves need to take a nap, so the rest of the mothers in the herd stand over them. Their shadows keep the babies cool as they snooze. The mothers keep watch for lions that could attack.

Mother elephants

Sleeping calf

Elephant sanctuary

What is an elephant sanctuary?

It is a safe place where elephants are protected. Sick elephants can be taken to a sanctuary, as well as young elephants who have lost their mothers. Once an elephant is old enough or well again it can be released back into the wild.

Handy noses!

Trunks are very handy. Elephants use them for holding and grabbing things, as well as greeting each other and fighting.

Search

Find out more about elephant conservation (keeping elephants safe) and how people can help them.

Why did elephants go to war?

Long ago, before the days of tanks and planes, elephants were sometimes used in wars. Soldiers were safer high up on an elephant's back, and it gave them a good view of their enemy's army.

Quiz time

Do you remember what you have read about elephants? Here are some questions to test your memory. The pictures will help you. If you get stuck, read the pages again.

3. How do baby elephants grow so strong?

page 9

4. Why do elephants pick up sticks?

page 9

1. Were mammoths woolly?

page 4

5. Why are tusks like weapons?

page 13

6. Can people ride on elephants?

page 14

2. What is a baby elephant called?

page 7

7. How much do elephants weigh?

11. Do elephants remember?

page 25

8. Are trunks sensitive?

page 18

12. Why do elephants march?

page 27

13. What is an elephant sanctuary?

page 29

9. Why do elephants chew bark?

page 22

page 23

10. Which birds stand on elephants?

Answers

1. Yes, they had long, woolly fur for warmth
2. A calf
3. They drink their mother's milk, which is the perfect food for growing babies
4. To flick flies away, scratch or doodle in the sand
5. Male elephants use them to fight each other
6. Yes, Asian elephants sometimes carry tourists
7. Males weigh up to 6 tonnes, and females weigh about half of this
8. Yes, trunks are very sensitive
9. Because it is full of goodness
10. Egrets
11. They remember where to find water and food, and may remember their dead relatives
12. Elephants march to look for food and water
13. A place where elephants are protected

Index

A
Africa 8
African elephants 6, 8, 21
Asia 8, 15
Asian elephants 8, 14, 15, 20, 21

B
baboons 23, 27
bark 22
birds 23, 27
blood 11, 25
bones 5, 19, 25

C
calves 7, 9, 13, 18, 22, 23, 25, 28
caves 5, 27
charging 23
circuses 21, 26

D
dinosaurs 5
Dumbo 17
dung 17, 27
dung beetles 17

E
ears 8, 12, 17, 18, 25
egrets 23
elephant sanctuaries 29

F
feet 19, 24
female elephants 15
fights 12, 13, 29
flies 9, 23
food 4, 9, 25, 27
forests 8
fur 4

G
giraffes 16
grass 7, 22, 27

H
heads 12, 23, 24
hearing 19
herds 7, 25, 27, 28
hunting 4

I, J
ice 5
insects 17
Jumbo 26

L
leaves 6, 7
lions 23, 28

M
male elephants 15, 21
marching 27
mating 21
milk 9
mother elephants 7, 9, 13, 23, 28
mouths 18
mud 17

N
noses 5, 18, 29

P
paint 5, 15, 20

R
remembering 25
rhinos 11

S
salt 27
skin 5, 8, 11, 17
smell 21
stampedes 13
sticks 9
suckling 9
swimming 9, 24

T
teeth 13, 19
ticks 11
tourists 14
trees 6, 11, 15, 22
trumpeting 10, 11
trunks 7, 8, 10, 11, 18, 19, 20, 21, 24, 25, 29
tusks 13, 23

V
vets 11

W
walking 13
war 21, 29
water 9, 16, 24, 27
waterholes 16, 17, 25
woolly mammoths 4, 5

Z
zebras 16